I0528655

ESTD 2017

KIDS LIGHTHOUSE

ALL FOR HIS GLORY

To:_____
_____
From:_____
_____

Every piece matters

ONE DAY, A BABY TIGER WAS CLIMBING A TREE.

HE WAS TRYING TO FIGURE
OUT WHERE HE FIT IN.

THE WORLD IS SO BIG, SAID BABY TIGER, AND I FEEL SO SMALL.

AS BABY TIGER WAS IN THE TREE, HE NOTICED SOMETHING STRANGE ON THE GROUND.

HE PICKED IT UP.

BABY TIGER WONDERED
WHAT IT WAS.

DETERMINED TO FIGURE OUT
WHERE IT CAME FROM,
BABY TIGER WALKED ALONG
THE PATH.

THE NEXT DAY, A BABY
OTTER WAS SWIMMING IN
THE RIVER.

SHE WAS TRYING TO FIGURE
OUT WHERE SHE FIT IN.

THE WORLD IS SO BIG, SAID BABY OTTER, AND I FEEL SO SMALL.

AS BABY OTTER WAS
SWIMMING, SHE NOTICED
SOMETHING FLOATING IN THE
WATER.

SHE PICKED IT UP.

BABY OTTER WONDERED
WHAT IT WAS.

DETERMINED TO FIGURE OUT WHERE IT CAME FROM, BABY OTTER WALKED ALONG THE PATH.

THE NEXT DAY, A BABY
BUNNY WAS HOPPING ALONG
THE FLOWERS.

HE WAS TRYING TO FIGURE
OUT WHERE HE FIT IN.

THE WORLD IS SO BIG, SAID
BABY BUNNY, AND I FEEL SO
SMALL.

AS BABY BUNNY WAS
HOPPING, HE NOTICED
SOMETHING ON THE GROUND.

HE PICKED IT UP.

BABY BUNNY WONDERED
WHAT IT WAS.

DETERMINED TO FIGURE
OUT WHERE IT CAME FROM,
BABY BUNNY WALKED
ALONG THE PATH.

THE NEXT DAY, A BABY KOALA WAS SITTING IN A TREE.

SHE WAS TRYING TO FIGURE
OUT WHERE SHE FIT IN.

THE WORLD IS SO BIG, SAID BABY KOALA, AND I FEEL SO SMALL.

AS BABY KOALA WAS SITTING IN THE TREE, SHE NOTICED SOMETHING ON THE GROUND.

SHE PICKED IT UP.

BABY KOALA WONDERED
WHAT IT WAS.

DETERMINED TO FIGURE OUT
WHERE IT CAME FROM,
BABY KOALA WALKED
ALONG THE PATH.

THE NEXT DAY, A BABY
PANDA WAS PLAYING
IN THE FOREST.

HE WAS TRYING TO FIGURE
OUT WHERE HE FIT IN.

THE WORLD IS SO BIG, SAID
BABY PANDA,
AND I FEEL SO SMALL.

AS BABY PANDA WAS SITTING THERE, HE NOTICED SOMETHING IN THE TREE.

HE PICKED IT UP.

BABY PANDA WONDERED
WHAT IT WAS.

DETERMINED TO FIGURE OUT
WHERE IT CAME FROM, BABY
PANDA WALKED
ALONG THE PATH.

THE NEXT DAY, A BABY
ELEPHANT WAS SITTING NEAR
SOME TREES.

SHE WAS TRYING TO FIGURE
OUT WHERE HE FIT IN.

THE WORLD IS SO BIG, SAID
BABY ELEPHANT,
AND I FEEL SO SMALL.

AS BABY ELEPHANT WAS SITTING THERE, SHE NOTICED SOMETHING ON THE GROUND.

SHE PICKED IT UP.

BABY ELEPHANT
WONDERED WHAT IT WAS.

DETERMINED TO FIGURE OUT
WHERE IT CAME FROM, BABY
ELEPHANT WALKED ALONG
THE PATH.

EACH ANIMAL FOLLOWED
THEIR OWN PATH.

THE TIGER FOLLOWED HIS PATH.

THE OTTER FOLLOWED
HER PATH.

THE BUNNY FOLLOWED
HIS PATH.

THE KOALA FOLLOWED

HER PATH.

THE PANDA FOLLOWED HIS PATH.

AND THE ELEPHANT,
FOLLOWED HER PATH.

EVENTUALLY...

THEY ALL REACHED THE
SAME PATH.

AS THEY MARCHED UP A
HILL...

THEY ALL REALIZED
EXACTLY WHERE THEIR
PIECES CAME FROM.

FROM A LOVING SAVIOR

WHO BELIEVES...

THAT EVERY PIECE MATTERS.

Then Jesus said to his disciples, "Whoever wants to be my disciple must deny themselves and take up their cross and follow me.

Matthew 16:24

IMAGINE THAT EVERYONE
WHO FOLLOWS JESUS HAS
A PIECE OF THE CROSS.
NOW IMAGINE HOW MUCH
YOU MATTER TO JESUS,
FOR HIM TO GIVE YOU THAT
PIECE.

Every piece matters

To see more books by
Kids Lighthouse, please visit
KidsLighthouse.com

www.ingramcontent.com/pod-product-compliance
Lightning Source LLC
Chambersburg PA
CBRC090826120626
46547CB00008B/615